LITTLE BITTY WITTY'S
(501 witticisms for families with little bitty's)

Written by Tracie McMeans

Published By:
BRIGHT BOOKS, INC.
2313 Lake Austin Boulevard, Austin TX 78703 (512) 499-4164

Printed in the U.S.A.

Copyright © 1994 by Tracie McMeans

All rights reserved. No part of this book may be reproduced or transmitted
in any form or by any means, electronic or mechanical, including photocopying, or by any information storage
and retrieval system, without permission in writing from the Publisher.

Library of Congress Catalog Card Number 94-72292

ISBN 1-880092-18-2

To Our Children, Our Future

There are many voices in this book contributing great ideas and encouragement, but they all want nothing but a bright future for their families. A special thanks to:

> KRISTEN—For giving me a reason to work harder at life, love more and for allowing me to be Queen.
> BILL—For making all my dreams come true.
> MOM—For persevering, the Monster Mash, my life and mostly for your love.
> NANA & TATA—For your unconditional love and sweet childhood memories (baby, baby ducks).

Dad, Sonia, Cindy, Aunt Marty #376, Uncle Manny & Aunt Dede, Aunt Jackie, Edna #399, Grandma & Grandpa, Bill Hanson, Laine Allen, Gary Buckley #497, Zina Kitowski #259, Mary Lorimer #147, Cindy Newton, Dawn Sudderth, Clarice Verdoorn #17, and Melissa Vogelsinger.

Introduction

This book is for anyone who wants, has or is having children, or knows someone who does. As a mother, teacher and volunteer on behalf of children's issues, I noticed we as parents need daily reminders of the simple, but not so little things to do for and with our children. This book has a few suggestions, big and little, with a few extras to help remind us of our responsibility to our children through love, common sense and humor.

We have been handed an enormous responsibility...our children. Along with this responsibility we have an opportunity to instill and keep values and morals in our lives and culture. It is our job to give them the strength to walk through life on a straight path and to always help others on their way as well.

The most precious gift we can give our children is time; the time we take to do things for them. Be it planning for their future world by being environmentally aware, to taking time out everyday just to be with them. Time is precious, but short, and we need to utilize it wisely.

I know from experience, being a parent is not easy, but it's the most important job we can have. I'm very lucky to have Bill, my husband, best friend and partner in life. We both know that God guides our hand daily and we are fortunate for the opportunity to help mold the future through our daughter.

1. Eat peanut butter & jelly sandwiches by candlelight.

2. Read with your children every day.

3. Teach them the importance of "Ma'am" & "Sir."

4. Teach them the magic words, "please" & "thank you."

5. Know your children's teachers by name.

6. When you ask your children how their day was, really listen to their answers.

7. Teach your children the <u>importance</u> of saying "NO" to drugs.

8. Teach them <u>how</u> to say "NO" to drugs.

9. Blow bubbles with them.

10. Go on their field trips.

11. Feed them nutritiously.

12. No book, movie, or story you've heard can even slightly prepare you for parenthood.

13. Make gelatin cubes and eat with your fingers.

14. Sing with them in the car.

15. Support and allow them to watch your local public broadcasting station.

16. Play hide and seek together.

17. Allow them to stay color-blind; children aren't born prejudiced.

18. If you don't smoke, your children may not start.

19. Worship together, other than on holidays.

20. You are not a bad parent if you gag while changing a dirty diaper.

21. Dance under a full moon.

22. Be a room parent.

23. Give them cookie cutters to use with their Play-Doh®.

24. Read one page of a classic novel every week.

25. Don't scold for accidents.

26. Post their artwork on the fridge.

27. Teach them about the dangers of strangers.

28. Keep a scrapbook of artwork from each child.

29. Take them to the zoo.

30. Make them eat breakfast.

31. Don't say words you would not want them to say.

32. Be forgiving.

33. Find another form of discipline other than spanking: "Time-Out" is making them sit in a quiet place one minute for each year of their age.

34. Laugh at all their jokes.

35. Never call them names.

36. Teach them to floss their teeth.

37. Make them wear shoes when playing outside.

38. Allow them to go barefoot on the grass in the spring.

39. Fly kites on a windy day.

40. Buckle them up, no matter how short the trip.

41. Hug and kiss them often.

42. They need to make their bed every morning; have them do it.

43. Set rules.

44. Help them live by example—yours.

45. Vote for their future.

46. Help them set up a lemonade stand in the summer and be their first customer.

47. Slow dance with them standing on your feet.

48. Dance to the "Monster Mash" at Halloween.

49. Set holiday traditions.

50. Give them homemade costumes.

51. Take lots of pictures and write the date on the back.

52. Bake and decorate cookies together.

53. Make lunch together and go on a picnic.

54. Wear their pasta jewelry proudly.

55. Teach them the state song, bird, flower, tree, and heroes.

56. Don't fry their foods.

57. Play on the monkey bars with them.

58. Make them write thank you notes; even crayon scribbles are appreciated.

59. Have them lick the stamps when you pay bills.

60. Before your child comes into your life, sugarcoat your words; they will taste better when you have to eat them later.

61. Teach them their phone number and address.

62. Teach them to dial 911 only for emergencies.

63. Feed them fruits and vegetables, fresh or fresh-frozen.

64. Control your temper. If you can't, call someone.

65. Don't let them drink from the container.

66. Talking to them about drugs is not introduction, it's prevention. Please don't be naive.

67. Send a love note to your child in the mail.

68. Teach responsibility by giving them chores.

69. Teach them to respect their elders.

70. Explain to them that dipping snuff doesn't make them a better cowboy.

71. Make them drink milk, even with chocolate, it's calcium.

72. Always tell them you love them, first thing in the morning and last thing at night.

73. After the age of two switch them to low-fat milk.

74. Read the Sunday comics with them.

75. Put all their handmade gifts in full view.

76. Have a favorite song—for the rest of their lives, whenever they hear it, they will think of you.

77. Keep yourself healthy for them.

78. The ultimate answer to paper or plastic: RECYCLE!

79. Make out a will. Keep it current.

80. Always give your baby-sitter plenty of information, including your address—if there is a fire will she be able to tell the fire department where you live?

81. Learn infant and regular CPR.

82. Respect their privacy.

83. Teach your sons to put the toilet seat down when they're finished.

84. Open a savings account for them and let them make deposits, no matter how small.

85. Teach them to be a good sport, they don't always have to win.

86. Make time to eat meals together.

87. Do not eat your meals in front of the television.

88. Teach them gun safety; you may not have one, but does your neighbor?

89. Teach them the "Star Spangled Banner" and to sing it with their hats off and their hands over their hearts.

90. Don't forget about the new big brother or sister in the house.

91. Teach them that "Everyone is responsible for his own happiness."

92. Teach them to respect other people's property.

93. Children do not need temporary tatoos.

94. Teach them right from wrong, then trust them enough to use the information you gave them.

95. You will always be their parent, but it's good to be a friend, especially when they become adults.

96. When you play Frisbee™ with children, aim at their knees.

97. Teach them not to stare at someone who is different; ask them if they have any questions, then answer the best you can.

98. If they ask "Why?" even for the 20th time, never say "Because."

99. Never compare your children.

100. When they bring in weeds pulled especially for you, put them in your best vase in the center of the table.

101. Teach them to turn out the lights when they leave the room.

102. Do not allow them to watch violent or adult-oriented television.

103. Teach them respect for all living things.

104. Always use sunscreen.

105. Reward your child not with things, but with praise.

106. If you are playing with your child, don't stop to answer the phone, this time is precious.

107. Never say "Because I'm your mother/father."

108. Get to know your children's friends and their parents.

109. When you catch your children behaving well, praise them immediately.

110. Reprimand in the privacy of their room, never in front of others.

111. Never make a promise you can't keep.

112. Never make threats you can't carry out. Children know. Besides, would you really cut out their liver and feed it to the birds?

113. Take them to the library.

114. High-five with them often.

115. Make their birthday a special day. Breakfast, lunch, and dinner should all be their choice.

116. Help them make a bird feeder out of a pine cone by rubbing peanut butter all over it, then rolling it in bird seed. Hang it where it can be seen during breakfast.

117. Boys can play with dolls, too.

118. Take family vacations that everyone will enjoy.

119. Help build a value-based society.

120. Never leave your children alone in the car.

121. Before your infant comes into your life, buy "Solve Your Child's Sleep Problems" by Richard Ferber, M.D. Trust me!

122. Never leave them unattended in water, even if they've taken a swimming class.

123. Install smoke detectors in your home.

124. Check your smoke detector batteries at the change of every season.

125. Always put life preservers on your child.

126. Enroll them in swimming classes.

127. A trip to the grocery store can be a learning experience. Ask them to count the items in the cart and name the color of things.

128. Always put paper on the toilet seat for them.

129. Fly paper airplanes.

130. Allow them to dress themselves. If your daughter wants to wear her swimsuit with red suede boots to the grocery store, let her.

131. Do not buy toys that promote violence.

132. Make your child wear protective gear when riding a bike, skateboarding, or roller skating, even small children riding in a wagon.

133. A great graduation gift: "Life's Little Instruction Book," by H. Jackson Brown, Jr. (Rutledge Hill Press)

134. Get them and keep them immunized.

135. Teach them not to litter.

136. Never flush a dead goldfish, a burial is more proper.

137. Tell your Maker "thank you" for them every day.

138. Sing "You Are My Sunshine" to them (and learn the second verse).

139. Never leave them unattended in the tub.

140. Get them a goldfish to take care of.

141. Put child safety locks on everything.

142. Do not take chances, put your cleaning supplies out of reach.

143. Buy outlet plug covers and use them.

144. Never give honey to a child under the age of one.

145. Allow them to take pictures—you will see the world from their point of view.

146. Teach them the Ten Commandments.

147. If the only thing preventing them from going to sleep is the monster under the bed, get some "Monster-Be-Gone" spray. In a small squirt bottle put a few drops of your perfume, fill with water, then spray around their room.

148. At least try to nurse your baby. God put them there for two good reasons.

149. Teach your daughter to mow the lawn, teach your son to cook.

150. Always buckle them into the grocery cart.

151. Teach them the facts of life; they don't get everything from the school film.

152. Understand AIDS so you can discuss it intelligently with them.

153. You cannot explain abstinence or condoms without discussing morals.

154. Their self-esteem is their most important asset, help them build it.

155. The "off" button on your television works. Use it often.

156. Hitting isn't necessary. It shows them that whoever hits the hardest wins.

157. Keep a few crayons and paper in your purse, you never know when you'll be kept waiting.

158. Never go shopping with your child if you expect to be carrying a lot of bags; criminals prey on people with their hands full, especially around the holidays.

159. Before you give your child a name, imagine how it will sound being yelled down the street.

160. Color with your children as soon as they can sit up.

161. Video games help with eye-hand coordination; however, you can get too much of a good thing.

162. Children who crawl think dog food is a treat.

163. Buy story books showing children of other races.

164. Feed your pet before introducing it to your new baby, it will be in a better mood.

165. Make puppets out of socks, but do not use buttons for eyes.

166. Start a neighborhood play group, it's free.

167. All of their dolls do not have to be the same color as they are.

168. Start a garden with your child.

169. BABY MONITORS! Keep a battery operated clock next to your child's crib—you can rest easier if you hear the ticking.

170. Don't worry, eventually they will stop sucking their thumb, even if it is because of peer pressure.

171. In the first week of life, a normal baby spends half of its waking hours crying.

172. If you feel there is a problem with your child, contact your doctor or local March of Dimes.

173. When you're pregnant and a stranger comes up to pat your tummy, tell them you charge $1 per pat. They'll probably keep their hands to themselves.

174. Start a compost bin.

175. If your daughter is begging to have her room painted pink, use "Pink Frost," it's subtle.

176. If your children are of the same gender and someone asks if you're trying for one of the opposite sex, ask them "Why?"

177. If you give clothes after a baby is born, buy a larger size than newborn.

178. If your child says, "I can do it," never say, "No, you can't." Let her try.

179. Finger-paint with your child.

180. When you're pregnant, do not change the cat's litter box.

181. Put healthy snacks on the bottom shelves of the fridge and pantry.

182. Never give clothes as a baby shower gift. Does anyone want to wear a green or yellow outfit for 3 months straight?

183. Change their toothbrush every 4 months.

184. Celebrate Big Bird's birthday. It's March 20th, the 1st day of spring.

185. Give old magazines and catalogs to your child to cut and paste with, it helps develop motor skills.

186. To help kids learn sequence get connect-the-dot color books.

187. Collect the Disney classics.

188. Collect a Christmas ornament every year for each child.

189. Play in the rain with them, but not if there is lightning in the area.

190. If your child has just gotten over a cold, replace or boil his toothbrush.

191. Try to read all you can about raising children and then trust your instincts.

192. Always cut hot dogs and grapes into quartered pieces.

193. Join the PTA.

194. At restaurants, don't order for them, they need to learn how to make choices; however, make them eat what they've ordered.

195. Encourage independence. Offer them a choice.

196. Install window guards even on the first floor.

197. Give them frozen yogurt instead of ice cream.

198. Allow them to take their own pillow on trips.

199. Put a big puff of shaving cream on a flat surface and let them play, it's easy to clean up. (Only for kids over two.)

200. Serve only 100% juice.

201. Respect their ideas.

202. Allow them to switch gears by giving them a 10-minute warning before changing activities, especially at bedtime.

203. Teach patience by being patient.

204. If it rains on your picnic, have it inside.

205. Teach your children the rules and etiquette of any sport they play.

206. Sparkle Play-Doh® is really cool.

207. Just say "NO" to "Beavis & Butthead."

208. Explain to them where butterflies come from.

209. Teach them to wash before eating.

210. Teach them to wash after going to the bathroom.

211. Broiled shark is healthy and tasty, and kids love eating things that could eat them.

212. Keep your child in easy on and off clothes when you are trying to potty train.

213. Leave time in their schedule for daydreaming.

214. Be honest. If they see you and your spouse in the tub together, explain water conservation.

215. Make a better tuna sandwich: tuna in water, no-fat mayonnaise, apple chunks, and pickles.

216. When you buy white canvas shoes, Scotch-Guard them before wearing them, they will stay cleaner.

217. Pots, pans, and a wooden spoon make the best toys.

218. Buy washable markers.

219. Buy lots of plastic Easter eggs. Put a penny or sticker in each one before hiding it. Like a woman at a sale, "It's the hunt that's fun."

220. When you mow the lawn, keep the kids inside.

221. Make popsicles using fruit juice.

222. Bake cupcakes in flat-bottomed cones and frost.

223. Frozen concentrated fruit juice is just as inexpensive as powdered drink mix, only healthier.

224. Use a shoe bag for all their art supplies and hang it over a door.

225. If you want to breast-feed, but your husband doesn't want to share you, tell him to wait.

226. If your husband wants you to breast-feed but you don't, explain to him that when he can produce milk, only then will your child be breast-fed.

227. Don't feel guilty, almost all parents change their mind about pacifiers.

228. Instill values: They need to have values so they can live them and defend them. It builds character.

229. Character counts!

230. Pack a healthier lunch box.

231. Cherrios in the toilet make great targets for boys during potty training.

232. Be an active volunteer, it teaches your child to help others.

233. Do not sell their fundraising items for them.

234. A child quickly realizes the value and power of whining.

235. Teach them to be accountable for their actions, thus helping them develop a conscience.

236. Ask the tooth fairy if you can buy back their first tooth.

237. Peer pressure starts much earlier than we want to believe.

238. Imagine what our world would be like if the next generation didn't have a conscience.

239. Never force your child to live out your unfulfilled dreams.

240. Always encourage.

241. Self-Esteem: The ability to deal with a situation rather than avoiding it.

242. Save a lock of their hair.

243. Spider Sandwiches: Peanut butter and jelly on whole wheat, cut into a big circle, stick raisins on bread for eyes, put on 8 pretzel sticks (4 on each side) for legs. The big square left is the web.

244. Every parent needs "The Right Start Catalog." To order call 1-800-548-8531.

245. Never kill a bug in your house when it can be captured and taken outside to be set free.

246. Admit it when you're wrong, they will respect you for it.

247. Poinsettias are pretty, but toxic; keep out of their reach.

248. Uninflated or popped balloons are a choking hazard.

249. Drapery and mini-blind cords are a strangling hazard.

250. Teach your children something about other religions.

251. Colored water in squeeze bottles makes great snow paint.

252. Leave cookies and milk out for Santa.

253. Help them learn the scientific names of dinosaurs.

254. The "Memory Game" really helps.

255. If you have Legos, buy a Lego Vac.

256. Never catch a firefly. The best part is guessing where they'll shine next.

257. Wooden blocks inspire.

258. They all need their own flashlight.

259. Save your egg shells, punch a hole in each end making one hole bigger, and blow the insides out. Let the eggs dry and save for Easter.

260. Buy lots of plastic food for their kitchen.

261. Get different hats for dress-up at a party supply store.

262. Teach the importance of exercise—go for a walk after dinner.

263. Teach them the real names of their body parts.

264. Give them a jump rope.

265. Play jacks with them.

266. Buy reusable juice boxes.

267. Disposable juice boxes are sometimes necessary.

268. Fold your hands, close your eyes, and listen to their prayers.

269. If you have a computer, teach them how to use it.

270. Buy sidewalk chalk.

271. Barney is a good guy.

272. Get a map of the United States and learn the states with them.

273. Learn the names of all the characters on Sesame Street.

274. Ice skate anytime: Tape paper plates to the bottoms of their socks and turn on the classical music.

275. Make musical instruments at home.

276. Drum: An oatmeal box and chopsticks. (Don't let them run).

277. Tambourine: dried beans inside 2 paper plates facing each other, stapled shut.

278. Cymbals: 2 cooking pot lids.

279. Horn: A paper towel tube.

280. Hint: Do not give 5 kids all cymbals at one time.

281. Teach the classics: "BINGO," "The Wheels On The Bus," "Old McDonald," and "If You're Happy And You Know It."

282. Everyone should get to know and love Joe Scruggs.

283. If you all travel often, get them their own suitcases.

284. Take them to the beach.

285. Give them a picture of you as a child.

286. Buy organic or scrub fruit and vegetables in soapy water before peeling.

287. Get them a bright raincoat for school.

288. Do not push them into sports.

289. Add shredded carrots and zucchini to spaghetti sauce.

290. Kids need fiber too.

291. Don't really need another toy? At their next birthday party, instead of a gift, have your guest bring a game to donate to your local Ronald McDonald House.

292. An empty cardboard box makes a great car, bus, or boat.

293. Take a picture of them in the tub filled with bubbles. You can use it against them when they are older.

294. Allow your child to overhear you praising her.

295. When they start to feel self-conscious about loosing their teeth, show them a picture of you with gaps.

296. Discuss everyone in the family album.

297. When setting up the nursery, buy a good mattress.

298. Wrap a gift in brown paper and let the kids decorate it with markers and crayons.

299. Go out to dinner around 5:00 p.m.; that's the children's hour.

300. Practice table manners at home, not just in public.

301. At holiday time, if it doesn't move, put a white Christmas light on it. They will always remember the glow.

302. Buy a crib that converts to a toddler bed.

303. Don't send them out in public with their name on their clothes.

304. Do not take your child to the toy store at Christmas, even the Grinch was never that mean.

305. Don't miss "The Little People's Guide To The Big World," volumes I & II, by Trevor Romain. (Bright Books)

306. Read "Green Eggs & Ham" very fast. It'll crack them up.

307. Carry a fake nose & glasses. If they throw a tantrum in public, put on said glasses and leave.

308. Always carry tissues with you.

309. Cut straws to 3/4" above the opening of the cup, thus preventing cuts on the roof of their mouth.

310. When you introduce new foods, do so at the beginning of the meal, when they are hungriest.

311. Mr. Rogers thinks you are special.

312. Even if she doesn't take ballet classes, get her ballet slippers.

313. Don't offer a reward for trying a new food; why would you be trying so hard if it tastes so good?

314. If they say "I'm mad at you," never say, "No you're not." They probably really are.

315. See the "Nutcracker" every holiday season.

316. Before leaving the house make everyone go to the bathroom first.

317. Let them set the table and don't worry which side the fork is on, eventually they will learn.

318. Tuna Bowling: seal boxes of cereal, pasta, or rice, stand in a Vee-shape, then roll a can of tuna at them.

319. Get a sock (no holes), add 1 cup dried beans, tie at one end—instant bean bag.

320. Buy a real Christmas tree.

321. If you know someone who is expecting another child and doesn't need baby items, give her a casserole shower.

322. Teach them to open the door for their elders.

323. Keep a nail brush in their bathroom.

324. It is impossible to predict intelligence based on when a baby starts walking and talking.

325. Check for ticks after campouts and hikes.

326. Get a small artificial tree for your children to decorate by themselves.

327. Learn together 1 new word every week.

328. Kids are like politicians when they want a pet: they'll promise to do everything.

329. Send homemade birthday invitations.

330. Great teacher gift: terra cotta pot—let your child paint the outside and add a plant; it's personal and inexpensive.

331. When you carve a pumpkin, scoop out the guts with your hands.

332. Practice Halloween safety.

333. On Halloween, go everywhere with them and carry a flashlight.

334. At a costume party paint faces instead of wearing a mask.

335. Check Halloween candy before eating.

336. Plant a tree the day your child is born and take a picture of him/her next to the tree every year.

337. If you have family out of town, sing holiday songs into a tape recorder and mail the tape to them.

338. In the fall, take a picture in a pumpkin patch.

339. In the spring, take a picture in the wild flowers.

340. Throw away broken toys; give away good toys they've outgrown.

341. If the siblings have duplicate toys, put their initials on them with red nail polish.

342. To encourage neatness, buy child-sized hangers.

343. Encourage their artistic ability, but not on the walls.

344. Crayon on your wallpaper? Rub off with a piece of white bread.

345. Keep a stain stick in your child's room, out of reach, and rub it on stains before tossing clothes in the hamper.

346. Every Sunday get the family together to plan a menu for the week. Kids should have a big input.

347. Clean out their room at the change of every season.

348. Have a cookie exchange party.

349. After the baby, plan a monthly date, a night out with your spouse.

350. Keep bath toys in a mesh bag and hang it from the shower head.

351. Install a hand-held shower head where you bathe them.

352. Make bath time safer: keep all bath products in containers that require only one hand.

353. Let your child pick flowers, press them, and send them to Grandma.

354. Encourage them to carry a handkerchief.

355. Explain to them that chewing tobacco doesn't make them a better baseball player.

356. Fireworks can be dangerous. Instead get a sheet of bubble wrap. Let the kids jump and ride their bikes over it.

357. Finger-paint with chocolate pudding on a plate.

358. Pancakes to go: pour batter into muffin tins. Bake 20 minutes at 350 degrees.

359. Use a bandanna as a bib.

360. Add confetti to balloons, inflate, and pop outside.

361. Keep the phone number for your local poison-control center handy, even in your purse.

362. Go to the lake or pond and feed the baby, baby ducks.

363. Explain the danger of matches and lighters.

364. Teach them to tell time; don't depend on digital watches and clocks.

365. Teething pain—chop a popsicle.

366. Busted lip—give them a popsicle.

367. Teach them to use coasters.

368. Keep a wet sponge in a Zip-lock® bag in the freezer; it's an instant soft icebag.

369. Let them drink soup from a coffee mug.

370. If your child has chicken pox, put calamine lotion in a bowl and give them a small, clean paintbrush to paint their pox. Parental supervision required.

371. When you go on a plane trip, have them take a backpack.

372. Watch the Olympics together and chant "U! S! A!"

373. Eat fishsticks by candlelight.

374. Teach them how to carry scissors.

375. Do not let them sit too close to the TV.

376. Kids do not know that goldfish can't swim on carpet.

377. Together give the dog a bath.

378. Chivalry should never be allowed to die.

379. Have a family night once a week. No TV; play games and read.

380. Ask your children if they like their baby-sitter.

381. Wear your seat belt while you are pregnant.

382. Writing is a lost art, help your child find it.

383. Keep the romance alive after your child comes into your life. Share a passionate kiss with your spouse every day.

384. Books make great gifts.

385. Never allow children to ride in the bed of a truck.

386. Not all girls like to wear dresses.

387. Teach them to use adults' last names.

388. No matter how you try to keep violent toys out of your home, your child can eat a ham sandwich into the shape of a gun.

389. Encourage them to play team sports.

390. Every time a baby cries, it does not need to be held, but make sure it feels loved.

391. The fear of God is theory. The fear of mom is reality.

393. While waiting for the doctor, ask for a pair of rubber gloves. Inflate and play games.

394. All children need a pet.

395. Hide eggs from the Easter Bunny, but teach them the true meaning of Easter.

396. Overpopulation of stuffed animals: hang them from the ceiling using cup hooks and ribbon.

397. Get involved and stay involved in their education.

398. Have a fire drill with an escape route and meeting place once you get out.

399. Encourage education.

400. Flannel sheets in the winter help you sleep better.

401. Whatever you feel are the biggest problems facing society today—illegitimacy, drugs, crime. Work as a family to end them all.

402. Everyone needs a bright red tricycle.

403. Get a highchair that requires one hand operation.

404. If you nurse your child in public, please be discreet, not everyone around you is comfortable.

405. Don't start putting them to sleep with car rides, you'll be sorry.

406. Play "London Bridge" and "Ring Around The Rosie" in the grass.

407. Make fruit kabobs using pretzel sticks, not toothpicks.

408. It really doesn't matter if they don't stay clean all the time.

409. Don't worry, they all smell like wet dogs at one time or another.

410. Tell stories about you as a child.

411. Let your parents tell the good stories about you as a child.

412. When eating out, check your children's food to make sure it's cooked properly. Before allowing them to eat.

413. Visit a fire station. Call first and take a fruit basket or cookies.

414. Pull over for all emergency vehicles.

415. Before sending them off to sell fundraising items, make them practice at home first.

416. Education—your children get out what you help them put in.

417. Don't wait until there's a toothache, go to the dentist before their first birthday.

418. Never ask, "Are you lying?" Explain the consequences of not telling the truth.

419. Teach them the unique sounds and actions of all animals.

420. If you hear your child say, "boys/girls can't do that," stop and ask, "Why not?"

421. Never take a sick child to a friend's house—what kind of friend are you.

422. Never take a sick child to school.

423. If your child complains of a headache—listen.

424. Your child should be allowed 1 or 2 items that he does not have to share, like a teddy bear or special blanket.

425. Check your home for lead and radon.

426. Protect your child, it's your job.

427. Help your child understand the true meaning of Christmas.

428. Balloons are invaluable at birthday parties.

429. Have a bicycle parade in your neighborhood on the 4th of July.

430. Read "The Book Of Virtues" by William J. Bennett. (Simon & Schuster)

431. Just because you don't like something, doesn't mean they won't.

432. Allow them to resolve their own disputes.

433. If you let them wear sunglasses, make sure they have UVA/UVB protection.

434. Teach them to use words, not fists.

435. Teach them to knock before opening a door, especially the master bedroom's.

436. "M&M's"® do melt in your hand after about 5 minutes.

437. Don't give them adult medicines.

438. Teach them how to clean house and cook.

439. Don't let kids share hats. Lice.

440. Think of others all year long, not just the holidays.

441. If you fly with your children, do not let them bother the person behind you.

442. Keep a few games and toys they can only play with on rainy days.

443. Children are having children! Do everything in your power to prevent this.

444. Adoption can answer prayers.

445. Homemade chicken soup works best for colds; it's the love you stir in that counts.

446. Own a large supply of cookie cutters.

447. If they have a diary, don't read it.

448. Don't go to bed with the kitchen dirty; mornings are tough enough.

449. Learn how to make old-fashioned candy apples.

450. TV can make you fat.

451. If the sun is shining and the birds are singing—GO OUTSIDE!

452. Compliment every family member at least once a day, not for how they look, but for who they are.

453. Stay out of their fights unless they are hurting each other.

454. They are children, not small adults.

455. Take them bowling.

456. Have a phone-in policy for kids who come home alone.

457. They want to play & you're pooped. Don't say "NO," play "Simon Says"— except you are always Simon.

458. There is more to pasta than elbow macaroni.

459. Don't allow them to use the microwave alone.

460. Don't force your children to be best friends.

461. Don't give them artificial sweeteners.

462. Don't expect the government to take care of them.

463. Our foster care system is overloaded, become a foster parent.

464. If you feel a child is being abused—report it.

465. THOUGHT: If someone corrected you as an adult as many times as we correct kids, how would you feel?

466. If you can, adopt a child with special needs.

467. Consider adopting an older child.

468. Preserve your wedding dress, she may want to wear it.

469. Put empty plastic produce bags in your diaper bag to store your dirty diapers (cloth or disposable) until you get home.

470. Keep an eye on the weather and be prepared.

471. Grow a sense of humor and keep it.

472. The best time to go to Disney World is the week after Easter.

473. The busiest, but most festive, time at Disney World is Christmas.

474. Even parents have guardian angels.

475. Children have guardian angels. They are called parents.

476. God never gives us more than we can handle.

477. Buy overalls in the fall and cut them off for shorts in the spring.

478. Breast feed before exercising or wait an hour after.

479. Watch John Wayne movies with them.

480. Read and watch "The Wizard Of Oz" with them.

481. Don't have more children than you can take care of.

482. Stay-at-home moms need life insurance; they are very expensive by the hour.

483. Everyone needs a rubber ducky.

484. Rubber stamps are more fun than stickers.

485. Buy rechargeable batteries.

486. A parent talking on the phone is an open invitation for a child to ask for something.

487. Don't let guilt motivate you as a parent.

488. Make eye contact when you talk to them.

489. Donate your kids' clothes after they've outgrown them.

490. Get a "No Whining" magnet for your fridge and point to it when necessary.

491. Start a baby-sitting co-op.

492. All children need a friend, be one.

493. Send a thank you note to the anesthesiologist who administered your epidural during childbirth.

494. Set up a quiet place for them to do their homework.

495. Build a tent with a sheet over chairs and eat lunch under it with them.

496. Take them to the state capitol.

497. It's not necessary to teach them how to burp louder than anyone else in the neighborhood.

498. Everyone should have a cowboy birthday party.

499. String cheese—calcium that's fun to eat.

500. Use their extra artwork to wrap small gifts.

501. Make sure they understand for the rest of their lives that they are responsible for their actions.